MW01625615
Meet
MASON
by Megan E. Rogers
Illustrated by Marina Saumell
To: Sincere
Thank you for
"Meeting Mason"

Meet Mason

Published by MasonStrong Publishing
Printed in the United States of America.

Illustrated by Marina Saumell

ISBN: 978-0-578-90865-6

To My Mason,

Thank you for teaching me to see with my heart and showing me the true meaning of unconditional love, patience and joy! You are the strongest person I know and you have forever changed how I see the world.

To My Mother Carol Rogers,

Thank you for walking this journey with me and being by our side every step of the way. You truly are a beautiful Mimi inside and out. There is no us without you and I am forever grateful for all that you do.

To Ethel McNichols,

As promised my first book is dedicated to you,
thank you for inspiring
and encouraging me to do this!
We Love you to life!

My name is Mason and as you can see there is something unique about me.

I walk with a cane to help guide me because I see differently than you.

It helps keep me safe and

I need to use it in all that I do.

My cane to me is like your eyes to you.

I also have to wear glasses to protect my eyes, I have many different colors and styles.

I go to school just like you, it is one of my favorite places to go.

I have an aid that goes with me, he helps with all that I do. He is very nice and will help you too!

I need extra assistance learning so I meet with special therapists that help me to grow.

I am also learning to read, but I use my fingers to feel braille words, would you like to feel too?

When I talk I sometimes have
trouble with my words but I
understand what you are saying to me!

I ♥
TACOS

Oatmeal and tacos are my favorite things to eat so you may hear me talk about them a lot!

I love music, I enjoy singing and listening to it. I hear some of my favorite songs every Sunday in church!

I like to go for walks, especially to the park, the swing is my favorite thing, what is yours?

I enjoy being outside in all the different weather and seasons because I like what each one brings!

I love the sun shining on my face,
the wind blowing against me,
even wet raindrops and
cold snow against my skin.

I enjoy it all and know the difference
by feeling it rather than seeing it!

I am sometimes loud but don't mind me I just get very excited and am expressing my personality!

COOL!!

I have a best friend and he is my brother.
If you are ever unsure how to treat me
just watch him, he will show you!

You are probably wondering why
I see and act different than you,
I was born this way, and I am blind.

Being born blind gave me a special ability to see with my heart!

I feel your kindness,
your concern,
your love!

You can tell by the smile I always have on my face that I am happy so please don't ever feel sad for me,

I just want you to understand me so we can be friends!

ROCK BAND

About the author

My name is Megan Rogers, I am the mother of 2 amazing boys who are 10 months apart. Mason, my first born is the inspiration for this book. He was born with an extremely rare genetic syndrome called Lenz Micropthalmia and is blind. My family's journey in the special needs world has been a roller coaster of emotions. I have experienced the most beautiful moments on this journey and some of the hardest days of my life. Through it all I can say my family is blessed. There is no handbook on raising a child with special needs but God has provided us with the most amazing doctors, therapists, and support groups. As Mason began to start school and be around other children whether it was church, the park, or anywhere I noticed they had so many questions and were just so interested in Mason and why he was different. I also found that most children had so much compassion for him.

I was given the opportunity at both Mason's school and our church to speak to his peers about being blind and its uniqueness and found it was very helpful. So I decided to write this book to help other children understand Mason or anyone else who may be blind or have special needs. I pray this book may help teach others to understand our children and treat them kindly. To show empathy but not pity. One thing I strive to teach Mason and others is that there is nothing he cannot do, we just have to find different ways to do them. I thank you for taking the time to Meet Mason and understand him.

Lenz Micropthalmia Syndrome

Mason was born with this extremely rare genetic syndrome. There are few reported cases of it worldwide. It is only found in males and the range and severity of it varies from case to case.

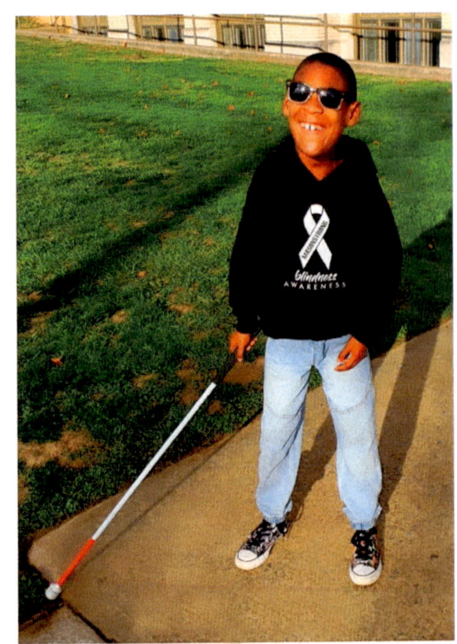

In Mason's case the way the syndrome has affected him is that his optic nerves never fully developed causing him to be blind and he has glaucoma. He also was born with heart defects that have been repaired through open heart surgery and he has a severe overall global developmental delay. The developmental delay has been more challenging than being blind for Mason, but he continues to progress every day. He also has some minor skeletal abnormities.
Mason has had many health issues and surgeries in his life, most recently his intestines twisted due to malrotation in uterus, this has yet to be determined if it is linked to his syndrome. When his intestines twisted he went into severe fatal septic shock, doctors had no hope for survival. It is a miracle that he is here today and God continues to shine his goodness on Mason and his life. No matter what Mason goes through he is always happy and that is such a blessing! He never gives up and he takes on everything being MasonStrong!

Made in the USA
Columbia, SC
14 June 2021

40044323R00020